Abiding In Him
A Guide to Drawing Closer to Christ

Cindy Hultine
Joy Martin
Stephanie Olson

Copyright © 2014, 2018 Hultine, Martin, Olson

All rights reserved. This book or any portion thereof may not be reproduced or used in any manner whatsoever without the express written permission of the publisher except for the use of brief quotations in a book review.

Unless otherwise noted, Scripture quotations are taken from the New King James Version®. Copyright © 1982 by Thomas Nelson, Inc. Used by permission. All rights reserved.

Scripture quotations marked (AMP) are taken from the Amplified® Bible, Copyright © 1954, 1958, 1962, 1964, 1965, 1987 by The Lockman Foundation. Used by permission.

Scripture quotations marked (NLT) are taken from the Holy Bible, New Living Translation, copyright © 1996, 2004, 2007 by Tyndale House Foundation. Used by permission of Tyndale House Publishers, Inc., Carol Stream, Illinois 60188. All rights reserved.

Scripture quotations marked (NIV) are taken from THE HOLY BIBLE, NEW INTERNATIONAL VERSION®, NIV® Copyright © 1973, 1978, 1984, 2011 by Biblica, Inc.® Used by permission. All rights reserved worldwide.

This book was compiled by Cindy Hultine with contributions from Joy Martin and Stephanie Olson.

ISBN: 0991454901
ISBN-13: 978-0991454907

Contents

Introduction

Jesus, the True Vine 1

Spend Time in His Word 4

Press in with Prayer 7

Learn to Worship 12

Exercise Trust 17

Surrender to Him 23

Turn to Jesus 29

Are You Ready to Be Set Free? 32

About the Authors 45

Introduction

So, what does it really mean to turn to Jesus? What does that look like in our daily lives? How can we learn what the Word of God says and implement it into our lives?

In this booklet, we hope to begin to answer these questions. It is our hope and prayer that God will begin to reveal to you His will for your life as you read through the following pages. We want to teach you simple ways to start reading your Bible, praying, and worshiping the Lord. We would like to share with you what we have learned about abiding in Christ.

This small book is only a guide; your real teacher is the Holy Spirit. Whenever possible, allow Him to lead and direct you. We want you to enjoy this journey; abiding in Christ will be the most exciting and fulfilling journey of your life.

A pastor was talking about spending time in the Word of God. He asked this very simple question: "What would our walk with the Lord look like if we prayed this prayer every day: 'Lord, give me a spirit of wisdom and revelation so I may know You more'?"

The same prayer that Paul prayed in Ephesians 1:17 for the Ephesians can become your prayer! And so, every day when you pick up the Word of God, pray that prayer. Ask God to give you a spirit of wisdom and revelation as you read His Word. Ask Him to open your eyes and heart to what He wants you to see in His Word, and pray for an understanding that goes beyond any limitations you might imagine. We will pray this with you on your journey of abiding in Christ.

Therefore I also, after I heard of your faith in the Lord Jesus and your love for all the saints, do not cease to give thanks for you, making mention of you in my prayers: that the God of our Lord Jesus Christ, the Father of glory, may give to you the spirit of wisdom and revelation in the knowledge of Him, the eyes of your understanding being enlightened; that you may know what is the hope of His calling, what are the riches of the glory of His inheritance in the saints, and what is the exceeding greatness of His power toward us who believe, according to the working of His mighty power which He worked in Christ when He raised Him from the dead and seated Him at His right hand in the heavenly places, far above all principality and power and might and dominion, and every name that is named, not only in this age but also in that which is to come. (Ephesians 1:15–21; NKJV)

-1-
Jesus, the True Vine

> Abide in Me, and I in you. As the branch cannot bear fruit of itself, unless it abides in the vine, neither can you, unless you abide in Me. (John 15:4; NKJV)

Keep Your Focus on Jesus
~ Stephanie Olson

Years ago my friend and I took our kids (five between us) to spend the day at a nearby lake. We had a great day playing in the lake and at an adjacent pool. At the end of the day, we all headed to the locker rooms to change clothes, with the entire group marching in a bit of a procession.

Everything seemed to be going smoothly until I did a head count and realized that Tessa, my three-year-old daughter, was missing. I instantly panicked as I thought about the massive lake that was just a few feet away from where we were. The first thing I did was attempt to look in the water for her, but the color of the water was muddied, and I couldn't see a thing.

I began to yell Tessa's name at the top of my lungs. The fear was so intense that I could barely breathe. When I realized she couldn't hear me, I ran back into the locker room area, which also held the offices. When I told the staff I couldn't find my daughter and needed help, the woman looked at me with a confused expression and said nothing—until my next tribal scream: "I need your help now!" That woke her up. Immediately, security became involved and began a search.

I was determined not to leave there without my daughter. I scoured the pool—nothing. I looked around the lake—again, nothing. I even ran back into the locker room thinking that maybe she'd found her way back to the rest of the group without noticing me—no such luck. All of a sudden, a woman came toward me with a crying Tessa in her arms. I practically melted on the floor in tears when I saw her.

Scooping her up in my arms, I hugged her and let her know in no uncertain terms that she had scared me beyond measure. The woman who found my daughter explained to me that Tessa was looking for us in the parking lot. She simply hadn't been paying attention, stopped watching us, and then stopped following us. All of sudden, she had become lost and didn't know where we had gone.

After I calmed down a bit, God used that experience to show me that we can often be like lost children in a massive area. When we are in a store or in any crowded place, I always tell my children: "If you can't see me, you are already lost." What happened to Tessa is exactly what happens to us during good and bad times in our lives. Her focus, as we were walking to the locker rooms, was no longer on me. Once she couldn't see me, she was already lost.

* * * * *

We must keep our focus on Jesus. When we stop focusing on Him, we can easily get lost. We can get lost in the shuffle, lost in the crowds, and lost in the emptiness of our lives. But with Jesus Christ, we can be assured that He can overcome absolutely anything.

What does it mean to abide? The definition, according to *Merriam-Webster's*,[1] is to "remain, continue, dwell, and stand firm."[1] Abiding, dwelling, remaining, continuing, and standing firm in Christ is what we need to do each and every day of our lives.

Read John 15:1–11.

Our job here on Earth is to abide. We need to abide in Him so we can go out to make disciples and love our neighbors as ourselves. When we abide in Him, everything else will fall into place. The fruit we bear—love, joy, peace, patience, kindness, goodness, faithfulness, gentleness, and self-control (Gal. 5:22–23)—will come naturally after some time. It won't happen in our own power, but rather by the power of Jesus Christ.

---

[1] Merriam-Webster's Collegiate Dictionary, Eleventh Edition (Merriam-Webster, Inc.) 2003

-2-
Spend Time in His Word

The Word of God, the Bible, is one of the primary ways God communicates with us. The Lord speaks to us through people and in our spirits but His Word was written to reveal His character to us and to express how much He loves us.

> For the Word of God is living and powerful, and sharper than any two-edged sword, piercing even to the division of soul and spirit, and of joints and marrow, and is a discerner of the thoughts and intents of the heart. (Hebrews 4:12; NKJV)

> All Scripture is God-breathed and is useful for teaching, rebuking, correcting and training in righteousness, so that the servant of God may be thoroughly equipped for every good work. (2 Timothy 3:16–17; NIV)

The Bible is God's true Word. Now, we think it's important to include a little Greek lesson here. Only one, we promise. The word *inspiration* in the Greek is *theopneustos*, which does not just mean the Bible was inspired like we might think of an author being inspired by something to write a good book. It means that it was divine inspiration. The word comes from joining the words *theos*, which means God, and *pneo*, which means breathe out. So, literally, we are told in Scripture that the words are breathed out by God and penned by man. When we understand the Bible is God's true Word, breathed by Him, we can then understand how vital His Word is to our lives.

Sadly, there is a tremendous amount of deception in the world today, even in the Church itself. Matthew 24:4–5 says, "Watch out that no one deceives you. For many will come in my name, claiming, 'I am the Messiah,' and will deceive many" (NKJV). The only way we can know if we are hearing the truth, even from well-known and well-respected pastors, is to know the truth of Scripture. If it is not in the Bible, it is not God's truth. We can only know the truth if we know what the Word of God says.

Even for mature Christians, knowing how to read the Bible can be daunting. Let's face it, it's a big book. We would like to offer you some ideas to help you get started.

- Use a Bible reading plan. (Several different plans can be found online.)
- If you are new to reading the Bible, start in the New Testament and read through the Gospels (Matthew, Mark, Luke, and John).
- You may choose to read for a set amount of time each day (for example, 15 minutes), or you may choose to read a certain number of chapters each day. But please don't allow yourself to view reading the Bible as a duty or a chore; rather, read as the Holy Spirit prompts you.
- Journal thoughts or questions you have about what you read so you can pray about them and

study them at a later time. Writing Scriptures down in a journal or on index cards is a great way to memorize Scriptures and store them in your mind.

There is no right or wrong way to read the Bible. Just try to read something from the Word of God each day. If you are just starting to read the Bible, however, we would encourage you to begin with the Gospels. Learn as much as you can about Jesus and His words. An amazing challenge is to read through the "words in red" five times. The words in red (included in some editions of the Bible) are meant to highlight the words of Jesus in Matthew, Mark, Luke, and John. It has been said that by the third time through, your life will change.

(At the end of this book, we have also provided Scripture cards of some of our favorite verses. You may cut them out and have them available to read throughout your day.)

-3-
Press in with Prayer

Prayer is one of the most intimate things we can do with the Father. Throughout the Gospels, we see that prayer was an extremely important part of Jesus' walk. He would spend hours in the middle of the night and early in the morning talking to His Father.

Jesus' disciples saw this man pray. These men had been praying all of their lives, but they saw something different in the way Jesus prayed. He prayed with a passion, a connection, and a fervor they had never seen before. And so they asked Him, "Lord, teach us to pray, as John also taught his disciples" (Luke 11:1; NKJV). Jesus, in turn, recites to them what we now recognize as the Lord's Prayer. In fact, Jesus tells us in Matthew 6:7–8, "And when you pray, do not use vain repetitions as the heathen do. For they think that they will be heard for their many words. Therefore do not be like them. For your Father knows the things you have need of before you ask Him" (NKJV). Instead, Jesus gave us this prayer as a model to learn how to pray.

Let's take a moment to look at this beautiful prayer in Luke 11:2-4 (NKJV) a bit more closely and see what we can learn. When we view this prayer as Jesus intended, rather than as a prayer to be repeated verbatim, we can grow immensely in our prayer life

"Our Father in heaven, Hallowed be Your name." Start your prayer with praise! His name is glorious!

"Your kingdom come. Your will be done on earth as it is in heaven." *It's not about us, Lord, not about what we want, but what You want.* Spend time praying for God's will to be done in your life in every aspect: your family, your ministry, your job, your nation, your schools, the lost, and on and on.

"Give us day by day our daily bread." *We trust that You will give us what we need each day.* What are your needs according to His will? What are the promises God has given you? Spend time praying about what He has for you.

"And forgive us our sins, for we also forgive everyone who is indebted to us." Okay, this can be a difficult one. *Forgive us, Lord*, yes, but we need to forgive others too. We can't come to the Lord while we hold offense against others. Really seek the Lord and ask Him if you are holding on to offense anywhere in your life. Allow God to heal that hurt and release that person, or thing, to Him (sometimes on a daily basis).

"And do not lead us into temptation, but deliver us from the evil one." If we hold on to unforgiveness, bitterness, and offense, we can easily fall into other sin. But God always provides a way out. What are the things that are keeping you from a full, intimate relationship with Him. Ask Him to help you that day with the things that you struggle with. Surrender those things to Him.

It's important to know what Hebrews 4:16 tells us—we can come boldly to the throne of grace. You can talk to God like you are talking to a friend. So often, we think we have to come to the throne speaking Elizabethan English and a highly formal tone. Nothing could be further from the truth. God desires us to come to Him as we are and talk to Him all day long. But it's also important to remember that God is a Holy, Sovereign God, and when we enter into His presence, we should enter with reverence and awe. Pray with passion and persistence and remember that our Father knows the things we need even before we ask.

> Now it came to pass, as He was praying in a certain place, when He ceased, that one of His disciples said to Him, "Lord, teach us to pray, as John also taught his disciples." So He said to them, "When you pray, say:
>
> Our Father in heaven,
> Hallowed be Your name.
> Your kingdom come.
> Your will be done
> On earth as it is in heaven.
> Give us day by day our daily bread.
> And forgive us our sins,
> For we also forgive everyone who is indebted to us.
> And do not lead us into temptation,
> But deliver us from the evil one."
> (Luke 11:1–4; NKJV)
>
> And when you pray, do not use vain repetitions as the heathen do. For they think that they will be heard for their many words. Therefore do not be like them. For your Father knows the

things you have need of before you ask Him. (Matthew 6:7–8; NKJV)

So I say to you, ask, and it will be given to you; seek, and you will find; knock, and it will be opened to you. For everyone who asks receives, and he who seeks finds, and to him who knocks it will be opened. (Luke 11:9–10; NKJV)

The Lord's Prayer is an incredible way to spend time in prayer. But we would like to share a few tips with you to help you develop your time with the Lord.

- Satan loves to distract us while we're having our devotional time; the phone will ring, we will check our email or get a text, or worse yet, thoughts will pop into our head of all of the things we need to accomplish in the day. Tip: Wait to check your computer until after your time with the Lord, and sit with a pad of paper and a pen to jot down any thoughts that try to take over your mind. Then you will be able to refer back to those "to-do's" after your time with God.
- Find a quiet place, if possible, away from noise and distraction.
- Instead of turning on the TV, turn on some worship music and spend that time praising the Lord.

- Don't neglect those moments while driving, getting ready for the day, showering, etc. to talk to God in prayer.

If you need further guidance, you may use the acronym "PRAY."

Praise: Praise God and thank Him for who He is and all of the good things in your life.

Repent: Confess your sins, ask for forgiveness, and then turn from your sins.

Ask: Ask for the things you need.

Yield: Wait and let God have a turn.

-4-
Learn to Worship

Read Luke 7:36-50.

I love this story of the woman who loved much. This woman only wanted to sit at the feet of Jesus and worship Him. She sacrificed money and endured humiliation and ridicule in order to worship Jesus. She didn't receive gain or glory, and she didn't seek those things either. She just wanted to honor and glorify the One who is worthy of that honor and glory.

Worship is not just something that happens on a Sunday morning while singing songs. Worship should happen every day, all day long. Worship is praising God not because of what He can do for you, but rather because of who He truly is. He desires consistent worshipers, praising His name through the good times and the bad.

We see this in the psalms David wrote. He was fleeing from Saul, who was trying to kill him. David pretended he was insane and then hid in a cave to escape a king who was hunting him down. Let's see what David says while he's under these conditions. He worshipped through these difficult times, and we need to do the same. Worship is a powerful tool.

Read Psalm 57 and Psalm 142.

Next, let's examine the story from 2 Chronicles. It is the story about a man who was in the midst of a battle. This man was a king, the king of Judah.

Read 2 Chronicles 20:1–20.

Here is King Jehoshaphat, who was just told that a great multitude of armies were coming to attack him and his men. He was extremely fearful. Try to imagine the fear you would experience if "a great multitude of armies" were coming after you. We're told that these armies were Moabites, Ammonites, and others from Syria, and they were ready to attack. That would put fear in anyone.

But look at what this king does; he doesn't do what we might expect him to do. We might expect him to call together his armies, plan a counterattack, or run for cover. But he does none of these things. No, in verse 3, we're told that the first thing he does is "set himself to seek the Lord."

King Jehoshaphat gathered all of the cities of Judah and stood in the assembly and said the following:

> O Lord God of our fathers, are You not God in heaven, and do You not rule over all the kingdoms of the nations, and in Your hand is there not power and might, so that no one is able to withstand You? Are You not our God, who drove out the inhabitants of this land before Your people Israel, and gave it to the descendants of Abraham Your friend forever? And they dwell in it, and have built You a sanctuary in it for Your name, saying,

"If disaster comes upon us—sword, judgment, pestilence, or famine—we will stand before this temple and in Your presence (for Your name is in this temple), and cry out to You in our affliction, and You will hear and save." (2 Chronicles 20:6–9; NKJV)

God responded by saying:

> Do not be afraid nor dismayed because of this great multitude, for the battle is not yours, but God's. (verse 15)

> You will not need to fight in this battle. Position yourselves, stand still and see the salvation of the Lord, who is with you, O Judah and Jerusalem! Do not fear or be dismayed, tomorrow go out against them, for the Lord is with you. (verse 17)

> And Jehoshaphat bowed his head with his face to the ground, and all Judah and the inhabitants of Jerusalem bowed before the Lord, worshiping the Lord. (verse 18)

This is so important to see. Jehoshaphat and his men had a battle stance; it was to worship the Lord. Their battle stance was literally on their hands and knees. When we are facing battles in our daily lives, regardless of what they are, we need to take our stance.

We need to worship. The heaviness of the attack can lift by worshiping the Lord, because the enemy cannot succeed when we are giving praise to the One True God.

Following are a few ideas to get you started in worship:

• Read through the Psalms (Psalms 34, 104, 136, and 145 are great places to begin).

• Thank God for who He is. He is the Alpha and the Omega, the Beginning and the End, the Great I Am, and the Creator of the Universe.

• Thank God for all the good things in your life, for He is the Creator of all things good.

• Listen to praise music or sing old hymns. The Internet can be a great resource if you don't have any praise music available to you. Or find a Christian radio station in your area and begin to listen to worship music in your car while driving.

• Just be in His Presence.

-5-
Exercise Trust

> And we know that all things work together for good to those who love God, to those who are the called according to His purpose. (Romans 8:28; NKJV)

> And the LORD passed before him and proclaimed, "The LORD, the LORD God, merciful and gracious, longsuffering, and abounding in goodness and truth, keeping mercy for thousands, forgiving iniquity and transgression and sin, by no means clearing the guilty, visiting the iniquity of the fathers upon the children and the children's children to the third and the fourth generation." (Exodus 34:6–7; NKJV)

A Story of Trust
~ Joy Martin

In April 2009, my husband Zach and I welcomed Julie Evelyn into our family, a blue-eyed, blonde-haired bundle of personality. Before deciding to have baby number two, we talked extensively about what expanding our family to four would mean for us. Justice was finally in school full time, and after years of split-shift parenting with me working days and Zach working evenings and weekends, we were finally both working normal hours.

After much consideration, we decided that I would quit my full-time job and look for freelance work after the baby was born. It wasn't an easy decision or one that we came by lightly. After all, it meant giving up almost half of our income, and with freelance work there is no guarantee there will be a next assignment. But, I felt strongly that God was calling me to stay home, and we decided that we'd just have to make it work.

The weeks following Julie's birth were really, really rough. And I'm not talking having trouble readjusting to a newborn rough. I mean they were the kind of rough where I didn't know how I was going to make it through the day. I won't go into details, but by early June things finally seemed to be looking up. I had been putting off going into the office and officially telling my supervisors I wouldn't be coming back from maternity leave—you know, just in case. But one Monday morning while I was praying, I felt a nudge that I needed to step out in faith and go have the talk with my workplace. I'm not sure why, but I decided that I would do it that coming Friday. I was excited and nervous all at the same time.

And then something happened that rocked my world. One afternoon that week I got a call from Zach saying he'd found a hard copy of an email that must have accidentally gotten mixed up in a pile of papers he'd been given by his manager. The email seemed to indicate that he would be losing his job. And although Zach went to his manager and talked to him about the situation, he wasn't able to get a straight answer. He wouldn't assure Zach that his job was safe, but he also didn't say anything to confirm our fears. We were left, well, hanging.

Needless to say, we found ourselves in a bit of a pickle. Our gut instincts told us that Zach would be losing his job on Monday, and I was planning to leave my full-time job on Friday. For those of you keeping track, that's me putting in my notice *before* we knew for sure if Zach would have a job come Monday. It was a rough week, to say the least.

I don't know how many hours I prayed that week or how many tears I shed, but I can assure you it was a lot. Should I keep my job so we had a safety net? If I did go back to work, what would we do with Julie— our newborn, breastfeeding baby whom I wasn't able to pump for? What would happen if we found ourselves without an income? Any income? Sure, Zach could find part-time work quickly, but we had no idea how long it would take to find a stable, full-time job as a heating and air tech, especially at a time when so many companies were unable to keep the employees they already had busy with 40-hour weeks. Logically, there was a clear answer. But God doesn't always operate in the realm of human logic.

I had trusted God for so many things. I had kept the faith through devastating situations, trusting that He would get me through and bring my family out of the pit stronger. But this? This made no sense. How could He possibly ask me to give up an amazing career that paid well, knowing that my husband would likely be out of work three days later? Surely God wouldn't do that, would He?

I ran every scenario in my mind. I figured that the best case scenario was that God was planning a miracle. I would leave my job, and God would reward my faithfulness by allowing Zach to keep his. That would still be a test, right? But the reality of the situation was that I had no idea what Monday held. God was looking me in the eyes and telling me to take a leap of faith. "Trust me, Joy. I'll catch you. I always have, and I promise in My Word I always will."

In Deuteronomy 31:6, Moses is speaking to the Israelites not long before his death. He is preparing them to cross the Jordan into the Promised Land with Joshua, and he says to them, "Be strong and courageous. Do not be afraid or terrified because of them, for the LORD your God goes with you; he will never leave you nor forsake you" (NIV).

And so, I made what was the hardest decision of my life. I emailed my supervisors and set up a time to meet with them that Friday afternoon. I cried on the way there, I cried during our meeting, and I cried on the way home. I was a ball of emotion—I was nervous, scared, excited, relieved, and conflicted all at once.

Now, it would be a lovely ending to the story to tell you that God gave us an easy way out by allowing Zach to keep his job. Wouldn't it? But Zach did lose his job.

Well, here's the kicker. God *will* catch you. He will prove faithful in all things—He promises us that in His Word. But that doesn't mean He won't let you experience the feel of the fall. I can tell you from firsthand experience that the falling is scary. But know this … the catch is indescribably amazing.

And as He promised, God did catch us. We had people who stepped in to help us out financially when we needed it most. I was able to freelance, and Zach qualified for unemployment and was able to find part-time work to get us by.

And two months later, God provided Zach with an amazing job—one that hadn't even been advertised, no less. But better than that, it's the first job that Zach has enjoyed. He is happier now than he's ever been. And were it not for that horrific fall, we wouldn't have experienced the joy of the catch.

* * * * *

We may not always see the big picture, but we can trust that God loves us and wants only the best for us. If we truly trust Him, we can rest and abide in Him and know that He will take care of things. In order to achieve this, you need to know who you are in Him and who you are to Him. You need to understand that if you are a child of God, you are His.

> And He said to me, "My grace is sufficient for you, for My strength is made perfect in weakness." Therefore most gladly I will rather boast in my infirmities, that the power of Christ may rest upon me. (2 Corinthians 12:9; NKJV)

> Trust in the LORD with all your heart, And lean not on your own understanding; In all your ways acknowledge Him, And He shall direct your paths. (Proverbs 3:5–6; NKJV)

"For My thoughts are not your thoughts, Nor are your ways My ways," says the LORD. (Isaiah 55:8; NKJV)

Have I not commanded you? Be strong and of good courage; do not be afraid, nor be dismayed, for the LORD your God is with you wherever you go. (Joshua 1:9; NKJV)

"For I know the thoughts that I think toward you," says the LORD, "thoughts of peace and not of evil, to give you a future and a hope." (Jeremiah 29:11; NKJV)

-6-
Surrender to Him

Finally, we need to surrender to the obedience of Christ.

Read Galatians 5.

A Story of Obedience
~ Stephanie Olson

I was driving in the middle of rush hour one morning, in the middle of winter, with my 18-month-old daughter in the back seat of my car. I was in a bit of a hurry, and it was cold. I looked over to my left, and on the sidewalk—on the opposite side of traffic—was a little boy riding his bike with no gloves. Every so often he would stop and try to warm his hands with his mouth.

I felt God speaking to me in my spirit saying, "Go give that boy your gloves." My reply? "God, I'm in the middle of rush hour on a two-lane road. How in the world would I turn around?" And yet, God repeated, "Go give that boy your gloves."

I continued to argue with God about how it was absolutely not convenient for me to turn around and give that boy my gloves. Do you know what? I didn't do it. I wasn't obedient. That moment has "haunted" me since that time. I will never know what I could have done to have blessed that boy, and I will never know how God wanted to bless me through that experience. But God always brings that to my mind when I'm debating whether or not to be obedient to Him.

* * * * *

Rules and regulations are critical in having a healthy relationship no matter whom it's with. If we want a healthy work relationship, we have to submit to the rules of the workplace. If we want a healthy relationship in a marriage, we have to submit to the rules of a successful marriage. If our children want a healthy relationship with us, they must submit to the rules we, as parents, set in our household. It is no different in a relationship with God. If we want to live a healthy and victorious life, we must submit our lives to Him.

Obedience requires boldness—when we trust that God loves us and has our best interests at heart, we can trust Him with all we do. He doesn't always ask us to do comfortable things, but I have never heard anyone say, "I was obedient to God, and I wish I wouldn't have been." God will never ask us to do something that He doesn't give us the strength, ability, or resources to do. Deuteronomy 30:11 tells us, "For this commandment which I command you today is not too mysterious for you, nor is it far off" (NKJV). In other words, if God commanded us to do something, it's not too hard for us when He gives us the grace to accomplish it.

It's not always easy being obedient, but 2 Corinthians 3:12 says, "Therefore, since we have such hope, we use great boldness of speech" (NKJV). We don't need to worry about what our friends will think of us or whether people will think we're "Jesus freaks." We can be bold in Christ, because we have the glorious hope that the Creator of the Universe loves us and we have eternal life with Him.

We need to surrender every aspect of our lives to God. The life of a Christian is not about religion. It is not just about going to church every Sunday and calling it good. God did not give us His Word—this living, active, alive Word—to give us a list of do's and don'ts. Jesus is not about rules and regulations. But He gives us His Word to show us the way to live and to have a life of victory.

Paul is telling us that we can be bold in Christ when we live our lives led by the Holy Spirit. We must surrender our sinful nature to God. We have an obligation to seek the Lord so He can do His part.

God calls us to live lives of righteousness and holiness. We are called to look more like Christ than the world. When we look like the world, what happens? Well, not only do people not see a difference between the world and Jesus, but what's even worse is that when we look just like the world, people don't want to follow Jesus at all!

Here's the grace part. God never intended for you to do any of this alone! You need Jesus. He wants us to have a relationship with Him. Jesus is real and wants to be involved in every detail of your life. He wants you to spend time in prayer. It's not necessary to have long, fancy, boring prayers. Just talk to Him as if He were sitting across from you at the kitchen table. Tell Him what's going on in your day, the details in your life. Tell Him what you're struggling with and that you can't do it alone. Tell Him how angry you are and why you feel the way you do. He wants you to come to Him with everything!

Jeremiah 29:13-14a says, "And you will seek Me

and find Me, when you search for Me with all your heart. I will be found by you, says the Lord, and I will bring you back from your captivity" (NKJV). He wants to set you free! He wants you to have freedom in Him! You can't do this on your own. You have to allow Jesus to take over. You need to say, I give up Lord, and I've tried to control it this long. No more. It's yours!

Hebrews 12:1-2 says in the New Living Translation, "Therefore, since we are surrounded by such a huge crowd of witnesses to the life of faith, let us strip off every weight that slows us down, especially the sin that so easily trips us up. And let us run with endurance the race God has set before us. We do this by keeping our eyes on Jesus, the champion who initiates and perfects our faith. Because of the joy awaiting Him, He endured the cross, disregarding its shame. Now He is seated in the place of honor beside God's throne."

2 Corinthians 5:17 says, "Therefore, if anyone is in Christ he is a new creation; old things have passed away; behold, all things have become new" (NKJV). We are no longer the same people we were when we accept Jesus Christ in our lives. We are new creatures with a new reputation. 2 Corinthians 5:21 says, "For He made Him who knew no sin to be sin for us, that we might become the righteousness of God" (NKJV).

Jesus was without sin, but He sacrificed His life and took all of our sins on Himself. Think about that for a minute. The sin that had been committed and the sin that hadn't been committed—He took it all on Himself. Think about some of the evils that are committed today. He took that on Himself so that *you* could have a relationship with Him and be the righteousness of God! The righteousness of God!

He humbled Himself by coming down to Earth as a man. Think about this for a moment. He is God! He came out of His "Godness" and put Himself into the body of a man to be fully God and fully man! Imagine the confinement He must have experienced. He did this so He could give you eternal life. He doesn't want you in hell, separated from Him; He wants a relationship with you.

But take hold of this part as well: "For we do not have a High Priest who cannot sympathize with our weaknesses, but was in all points tempted as we are, yet without sin. Let us therefore come boldly to the throne of grace, that we may obtain mercy and find grace to help in time of need" (Heb. 4:15-16; NKJV).

It's all about His mercy and grace. He loves you! And know this: if you were the only person on the face of Earth, He would have still died for you. Because He loves *you*!

There are some of you who are afraid to get close to God by reading His Word and spending time in prayer and worship because you are afraid that He might just ask you to surrender some things. Maybe He'll ask you to stop that relationship that is wrong or not good for you. Maybe He'll ask you to stop drinking or doing drugs and find some help. Maybe He'll ask you to stop eating to excess and start exercising. Maybe He'll ask you to stop gossiping. Maybe He'll ask you to forgive that person you don't want to forgive.

No one says that walking a life with Jesus and living a life of victory out of your addictions, pain, and bondage is easy. It's not easy; it's a lot of hard work. But God will not ask us to do anything that is not possible. He won't do it magically for us either. We can also promise you after the hard work, living a life of victory feels better. We promise.

God does require obedience from us. Not because He wants us to be like robots doing what He wants us to do. No, He requires obedience because He loves us and wants the best for us. He knows that all of those things I just mentioned, and anything else that you can come up with, hurt us and hurt those we love. When we are involved in things contrary to His Word, it is not God's best for us.

1 John 4:4 says, "You are of God, little children, and have overcome them, because He who is in you is greater than he who is in the world" (NKJV). If you have accepted Jesus as your Savior and have God living in you, you can overcome anything because God is greater than Satan! You have the battle conqueror living inside you! Win that battle!

We can honestly say that our past has not been easy. We have felt unworthy, a tremendous amount of shame, and truly lost at times. But we would never go back and change a single moment, because He can use that pain from the past and turn it into something beautiful to glorify Him. God wastes nothing! What Satan intends for harm, God can use for good and for His glory!

Turn to Jesus
by Stephanie Olson

What are you suffering with? A broken heart? Turn to Jesus.

What are you suffering with? Anger? Turn to Jesus.

What are you suffering with? Bitterness and hate? Turn to Jesus.

What are you suffering with? The loss of someone you love? Turn to Jesus.

What are you suffering with? The pain of an addiction? Turn to Jesus.

What are you suffering with? A destructive relationship? Turn to Jesus.

What are you suffering with? A feeling of loneliness? Turn to Jesus.

What are you suffering with? Not fitting in? Turn to Jesus.

What are you suffering with? Not being able to put food on your table? Turn to Jesus.

Does that sound too simple? Can Jesus really heal all hurts? Yes it does, and yes He can.

It's about surrendering to the One who can calm any storm. "He calms the storm, so that its waves are still" (Psalm 107:29; NKJV).

It's about knowing we can't do it on our own and saying to Jesus, "Lord, save me!" Jesus immediately reaches out His hand and catches us (Matthew 14:30 – 31). It's about turning it all over to Jesus.

So, when you are suffering with a broken heart, turn to Jesus. "He heals the brokenhearted and binds up their wounds" (Psalm 147:3; NKJV).

When you are suffering with anger, turn to Jesus. "Though I walk in the midst of trouble, You will revive me; You will stretch out Your hand against the wrath of my enemies, and Your right hand will save me" (Psalm 138:7; NKJV).

When you are suffering with bitterness and hate, turn to Jesus. "Then Jesus said, 'Father, forgive them, for they do not know what they do'" (Luke 23:34; NKJV).

When you are suffering with the loss of someone you love, turn to Jesus. "Blessed are those who mourn, for they will be comforted" (Matthew 5:4 NKJV).

When you are suffering with the pain of an addiction, turn to Jesus. "This means that anyone who belongs to Christ has become a new person. The old life is gone; a new life has begun" (2 Corinthians 5:17; NLT)!

When you are suffering with a destructive relationship, turn to Jesus. "God is faithful (reliable, trustworthy, and therefore ever true to His promise, and He can be depended on); by Him you were called into companionship and participation with His Son, Jesus Christ our Lord" (1 Corinthians 1:9; AMP).

When you are suffering with a feeling of loneliness, turn to Jesus. "I will never leave you nor forsake you" (Hebrews 13:5; Deuteronomy 31:6; NKJV).

When you are suffering with not fitting in, turn to Jesus. "And we know that all things work together for good to those who love God, to those who are the called according to His purpose" (Romans 8:28; NKJV).

When you are suffering with not being able to put food on your table, turn to Jesus. "I lift up my eyes to the mountains—where does my help come from? My help comes from the LORD, the Maker of heaven and earth" (Psalm 121:1–2; NIV).

Turn to Jesus! "Come to Me, all you who are weary and burdened, and I will give you rest. Take My yoke upon you and learn from Me, for I am gentle and humble in heart, and you will find rest for your souls. For My yoke is easy and My burden is light" (Matthew 11:28–30; NIV).

Are You Ready to Be Set Free?

Having a personal relationship with Jesus Christ is so much more than a "religion." God sent His only Son to die for you! Even if you were the only one on Earth, God would have sent Jesus to sacrifice His life for you because He loves you!

Salvation is a free gift. There is no amount of work that you can do to earn your way into God's grace. God's grace is given freely—all you need to do is receive it. If you want a personal relationship with Christ, please follow these simple steps.

- Recognize that you are a sinner and that Jesus Christ is the only path to salvation.
- Spend some time alone with God—repent of your past sins and ask God to forgive you. To repent simply means to turn away from your old life and sinful ways and turn toward Christ.
- Say yes to Jesus. The God of all things wants to be a part of your life. Make Jesus the Lord of your life.

That's all you need to do. Personalize your new relationship by talking to Him daily through prayer and by spending time in His Word, the Bible.

"I am the true vine, and My Father is the vinedresser. [2] Every branch in Me that does not bear fruit He takes away; and every branch that bears fruit He prunes, that it may bear more fruit. [3] You are already clean because of the word which I have spoken to you. [4] Abide in Me, and I in you. As the branch cannot bear fruit of itself, unless it abides in the vine, neither can you, unless you abide in Me.

[5] "I am the vine, you are the branches. He who abides in Me, and I in him, bears much fruit; for without Me you can do nothing. [6] If anyone does not abide in Me, he is cast out as a branch and is withered; and they gather them and throw them into the fire, and they are burned. [7] If you abide in Me, and My words abide in you, you will ask what you desire, and it shall be done for you. [8] By this My Father is glorified, that you bear much fruit; so you will be My disciples.

[9] "As the Father loved Me, I also have loved you; abide in My love. [10] If you keep My commandments, you will abide in My love, just as I have kept My Father's commandments and abide in His love.

(John 15:1-10; NKJV)

"And we know that all things work together for good to those who love God, to those who are the called according to His purpose."
Romans 8:28 (NKJV)

"'For My thoughts are not your thoughts, Nor are your ways My ways,' says the LORD." Isaiah 55:8 (NKJV)

"For the LORD does not see as man sees; for man looks at the outward appearance, but the LORD looks at the heart."
1 Samuel 16:7b (NKJV)

"Come to Me, all you who labor and are heavy laden, and I will give you rest. Take My yoke upon you and learn from Me, for I am gentle and lowly in heart, and you will find rest for your souls. For My yoke is easy and My burden is light."
Matthew 11:28-30 (NKJV)

"Have I not commanded you? Be strong and of good courage; do not be afraid, nor be dismayed, for the Lord your God is with you wherever you go."
Joshua 1:9 (NKJV)

"Trust in the Lord with all your heart, and lean not on your own understanding; in all your ways acknowledge Him, and He shall direct your paths."
Proverbs 3:5-6 (NKJV)

"Be anxious for nothing, but in everything by prayer and supplication, with thanksgiving, let your requests be made known to God and the peace of God, which surpasses all understanding, will guard your hearts and minds through Christ Jesus."
Philippians 4:6-7 (NKJV)

"Finally, brethren, whatever things are true, whatever things are noble, whatever things are just, whatever things are pure, whatever things are lovely, whatever things are of good report, if there is any virtue and if there is anything praiseworthy—meditate on these things."
Philippians 4:8 (NKJV)

"Cast your burden on the LORD, and He shall sustain you; He shall never permit the righteous to be moved."
Psalm 55:22 (NKJV)

> "I can do all things through
> Christ who strengthens me."
> Philippians 4:13 (NKJV)

> Let the words of my mouth and the meditation of my
> heart be acceptable in Your sight, O Lord, my
> strength and my Redeemer."
> Psalm 19:14 (NKJV)

> "Call to Me, and I will answer you, and show you great
> and mighty things, which you do not know."
> Jeremiah 33:3 (NKJV)

> "Your word is a lamp to my feet and a
> light to my path."
> Psalm 119:105 (NKJV)

> "My brethren, count it all joy when you fall into various trials, knowing that the testing of your faith produces patience. But let patience have its perfect work, that you may be perfect and complete, lacking nothing."
> James 1:2-4 (NKJV)

> "And you will seek Me and find Me, when you search for Me with all your heart."
> Jeremiah 29:13 (NKJV)

About the Authors

Cindy Hultine, Joy Martin, and Stephanie Olson are an active part of the leadership team for Set Me Free Ministries®, based in Omaha, Nebraska.

Set Me Free Ministries began as a desire to see Christians put down the facade of "being religious" and truly be "real" with both Christians and non-Christians alike—the idea of a world in which Christians live by the fruit of the Spirit and walk in love. Years later that desire was combined with a deep burden for women (and men) who find themselves in spiritual bondage. This bondage may be huge, such as abuse or alcoholism, or it may be what some might consider smaller, such as being a mom and struggling with coping day to day with the kids.

Set Me Free Ministries has a burden for those who need to understand that although salvation is a gift, living your life in victory takes work, and it can only be done by turning your life and will completely over to Christ. So often, we are taught that Christ can set us free, but we are not always taught how that happens. So how do we walk in victory?

Our ministry is committed to teaching people how to live victoriously on a daily basis. Our goal is to help you get everything out of life that Christ has to offer.

Stephanie Olson Speaking & Consulting
P.O. Box 223
Omaha, Nebraska 68010
402-915-0511
www.stephanieolson.com

www.ingramcontent.com/pod-product-compliance
Lightning Source LLC
Chambersburg PA
CBHW061345040426
42444CB00011B/3091